JAMES

FAITH THAT WORKS

ANDREW T. &
PHYLLIS J.
LE PEAU

9 STUDIES
FOR INDIVIDUALS
OR GROUPS

Life
Builder
Study

INTER-VARSITY PRESS
36 Causton Street, London SW1P 4ST, England
Email: ivp@ivpbooks.com
Website: www.ivpbooks.com

Originally published in the United States of America in the LifeGuide® Bible Studies series in 1987 by InterVarsity Press, Downers Grove, Illinois
Second edition published 1999
First published in Great Britain by Scripture Union in 1999
Second edition published 2016
This edition published in Great Britain by Inter-Varsity Press 2018

British Library Cataloguing-in-Publication Data
A catalogue record for this book is available from the British Library.

ISBN: 978–1–78359–798–7

Printed in Great Britain by Ashford Colour Press Ltd, Gosport, Hampshire

Inter-Varsity Press publishes Christian books that are true to the Bible and that communicate the gospel, develop discipleship and strengthen the church for its mission in the world.

IVP originated within the Inter-Varsity Fellowship, now the Universities and Colleges Christian Fellowship, a student movement connecting Christian Unions in universities and colleges throughout Great Britain, and a member movement of the International Fellowship of Evangelical Students. Website: www.uccf.org.uk. That historic association is maintained, and all senior IVP staff and committee members subscribe to the UCCF Basis of Faith.

Contents

GETTING THE MOST OUT OF *JAMES* ———————— 5

1 James 1:1-18   **Dependable or Double-minded** – 10

2 James 1:19-27   **Words, Words, Words** ———— 13

3 James 2:1-13   **Who's the Judge?** ———————— 16

4 James 2:14-26   **Just Works** ———————— 19

5 James 3:1-12   **On Preventing Forest Fires** —— 22

6 James 3:13—4:10   **Makers & Breakers of Peace** —— 26

7 James 4:11-17   **Getting Perspective** ———————— 29

8 James 5:1-11   **What Awaits** ———————— 33

9 James 5:12-20   **Becoming Whole** ———————— 37

Leader's Notes ———————————————— 41

Getting the Most Out of *James*

Unlike most books of the New Testament, the letter of James is best known for the people who don't like it. It's seen as a scalawag among the obviously Christ-centered letters of Paul and the love-concerned writings of John. People like love. They like Christ. They don't like James.

James is harsh and dogmatic. We feel the sting of his words even today—"Don't be deceived," "You foolish person," "You adulterous people," "Now listen." We find James hard to take for good reason.

Of all the people who do not like James, Martin Luther is probably the most famous. Compared to the other solid New Testament writings, James, he felt, was full of straw—empty, hollow. He virtually relegated the letter to a position of lesser Scripture. He believed that it taught salvation by works. And that would never do for Martin "Salvation-by-Grace-Alone" Luther. Because of Luther's feelings and those of others like him, Protestant Christians have tended to ignore this book.

Yet the early church saw it as a book bearing apostolic authority and, more importantly, as a book that bore God's authority. James spoke a needed and empowered word to the churches. Thus it was included in the New Testament canon alongside Paul and John, carrying equal weight with their writings. Because it has been avoided and because it bears the full force of God's Word, James deserves our special study.

And what does it have to tell us? James is practical. Take problems. James knows nobody's life is perfect. So he doesn't tell us how to live trouble free, but how to live when troubles hit. Do we complain? Or do we use them as an opportunity for growth?

Take words. We all talk. And sometimes we say things we wish we hadn't. James helps us use words more carefully, more constructively. Do they hurt others? Do they advance God's kingdom? Are they truthful? Are they loving?

Take money. It flows around us (despite our protestations concerning tight budgets and taxes). Do we withhold it when others are in need? Do we put more value on worldly things than on the things of God?

Take time. If we have enough money, we know we never have enough time. We do all we can to get the most out of each hour of each day, filling our calendars with activity. But do we miss God's will and perspective in the midst of our schedule making?

James is practical—maybe too practical! So expect this study to be difficult—not because it will be hard to understand but because it will be all too easy to understand.

Who is this fellow James who makes us so uncomfortable? There are several people in the New Testament called James, including two apostles. Though they have never been completely certain, most church scholars have believed that a third man, James the brother of Jesus (Matthew 13:55; Mark 6:3), wrote this letter. While he probably rejected Jesus during his earthly ministry (along with the others in Jesus' family) James certainly started following Jesus after his resurrection. In fact, James soon became the head of the church in Jerusalem.

He probably led the first church council in Jerusalem (Acts 15), which decided that Gentiles did not have to become Jews before they could be saved. This is an important factor in assessing James's view of faith and works (which is to be noted in light of 2:14-26).

Yet James was aware of the very Jewish make-up of the church in Jerusalem and required Paul to squelch the rumor that he, Paul, was telling Jews to abandon the law of Moses. James himself apparently followed Jewish law closely, enough so that he was known as James the Just. He died a martyr in A.D. 62.

James addresses his letter to "the twelve tribes scattered among the nations." The twelve tribes could refer to Jewish Christians which through exile, enslavement and trade were spread throughout the entire Mediterranean basin. More likely it refers simply to Christians since the New Testament compares the church to Israel (Galatians 6:16 RSV; 1 Peter 2:9-10). In any case, the letter is not addressed to one specific congregation, as Paul's letters were. It is therefore called a general, or catholic, epistle.

The purpose of this guide is to help you face squarely James's call for a consistent Christian life, for a practical faith. We seek to do this through nine studies each covering about half a chapter each. This may not seem like much, but James's proverb-like compactness calls for it. You may not necessarily like James when you finish. But it is our prayer that through it God will give you a faith that works.

Suggestions for Individual Study

1. As you begin each study, pray that God will speak to you through his Word.

2. Read the introduction to the study and respond to the personal reflection question or exercise. This is designed to help you focus on God and on the theme of the study.

3. Each study deals with a particular passage—so that you can delve into the author's meaning in that context. Read and reread the passage to be studied. If you are studying a book, it will be helpful to read through the entire book prior to the first study. The questions are written using the language of the New International Version, so you may wish to use that version of the Bible. The New Revised Standard Version is also recommended.

4. This is an inductive Bible study, designed to help you discover for yourself what Scripture is saying. The study includes three types of questions. *Observation* questions ask about the basic facts: who, what when, where and how. *Interpretation* questions delve into the meaning of the passage. *Application* questions help you discover the implications of the text for growing in Christ. These three keys unlock the treasures of Scripture.

Write your answers to the questions in the spaces provided or in a personal journal. Writing can bring clarity and deeper understanding of yourself and of God's Word.

5. It might be good to have a Bible dictionary handy. Use it to look up any unfamiliar words, names or places.

6. Use the prayer suggestion to guide you in thanking God for what you have learned and to pray about the applications that have come to mind.

7. You may want to go on to the suggestion under "Now or Later," or you may want to use that idea for your next study.

Suggestions for Members of a Group Study

1. Come to the study prepared. Follow the suggestions for individual study mentioned above. You will find that careful preparation will greatly enrich your time spent in group discussion.

2. Be willing to participate in the discussion. The leader of your group will not be lecturing. Instead, he or she will be encouraging the members of the group to discuss what they have learned. The leader will be asking the questions that are found in this guide.

3. Stick to the topic being discussed. Your answers should be based on the verses which are the focus of the discussion and not on outside authorities such as commentaries or speakers. These studies focus on a particular passage of Scripture. Only rarely should you refer to other portions of the Bible. This allows for everyone to participate in in-depth study on equal ground.

4. Be sensitive to the other members of the group. Listen attentively when they describe what they have learned. You may be surprised by their insights! Each question assumes a variety of answers. Many questions do not have "right" answers, particularly questions that aim at meaning or application. Instead the questions push us to explore the passage more thoroughly.

When possible, link what you say to the comments of others. Also, be affirming whenever you can. This will encourage some of the more hesitant members of the group to participate.

5. Be careful not to dominate the discussion. We are sometimes so eager to express our thoughts that we leave too little opportunity for others to respond. By all means participate! But allow others to also.

6. Expect God to teach you through the passage being discussed and through the other members of the group. Pray that you will have an enjoyable and profitable time together, but also that as a result of the study you will find ways that you can take action individually and/or as a group.

7. Remember that anything said in the group is considered confidential and should not be discussed outside the group unless specific permission is given to do so.

8. If you are the group leader, you will find additional suggestions at the back of the guide.

1

Dependable or Double-minded?

James 1:1-18

No pain. No gain. Or so the saying goes. Athletes remind themselves of this to get their best possible performance. Sometimes they have to go through grueling training. Without it, there is no improvement. James suggests it is the same for Christians.

GROUP DISCUSSION. "Getting in shape is simple. Just eat right and exercise regularly." Why do you find this easier said than done?

PERSONAL REFLECTION. Think about when you have been in great shape physically. How does this compare and contrast to being in good shape spiritually?

In this study we will look at the importance of perseverance when we face trials and temptations. *Read James 1:1-18.*

---

1. What are the different situations described in this passage in which you see the need for Christians to persevere?

2. How do you respond to the idea that we should "consider it pure joy" whenever we "face trials of many kinds" (v. 2)?

_____

3. How are perseverance and maturity developed in us by enduring trials (vv. 3-4)?

_____

4. What difficult experiences have increased your perseverance and maturity?

_____

5. How might trials expose our need for God's wisdom (v. 5)?

_____

6. Under pressure, how does the faithful Christian (vv. 5-6) contrast with the person described in verses 6-8?

_____

7. In the context of trials and perseverance, why does James contrast rich and poor Christians (vv. 9-11)?

_____

8. In what ways do you tend to rely on your possessions?

9. How are temptations different from trials (vv. 2-16)?

10. What role does God play when we face trials and when we face temptations (vv. 2-16)?

11. How is God the ultimate example of goodness and dependability (vv. 16-18)?

How is this a source of joy and hope for you?

12. Think of trials or temptations you are currently facing. How can this passage encourage you to depend on God?

Talk to God about your trials and temptations and your need for his wisdom in those situations. Ask him to help you to learn to persevere and to be like him in his goodness and dependability.

Now or Later

One of the best ways to appreciate God's dependability is to recall the different ways he has shown his faithfulness in the past. Make a list of the ways you have seen God's reliability at work. Take time to thank and praise him for his steadfast love.

2

Words, Words, Words

We all do it. It's as common as flies around a horse. While someone else is talking, we're thinking about what we're going to say next instead of considering what is being said to us. We know others are worth more care and attention. But the habit is hard to break. God wants us to slow down and listen too. But even when we've really listened to him, we're still not done.

GROUP DISCUSSION. Really understanding each other is tough even when we understand the words people use. Remember the dictionary game? Each person makes up a definition of an unusual word and writes it on a piece of paper. The leader writes down the real definition and then reads what everyone has written. Each person in the group tries to guess which one is right. Try one or two rounds with some of the following words: *oviparous, foraminifer, isochroous* or *bersagliere*. (The real definitions are in the leaders notes—no peeking!)

PERSONAL REFLECTION. Think about a specific situation in which you were not pleased with how you listened to someone else. Think of another situation in which you were not pleased with how someone listened to you. Why is it so difficult to be a good listener?

This study gives us practical help on listening to others and to the Word as well as help on how to put the Word into practice. *Read James 1:19-27.*

---

1. What do you learn about what God desires from us from these verses?

---

2. How can being quick to listen and slow to speak help us be slow to become angry (v. 19)?

---

3. How could the commands in verse 19 affect the way your small group or Christian fellowship interacts?

---

4. When have you experienced the truth that "man's anger does not bring about the righteous life that God desires" (v. 20)?

---

5. James tells us that God's Word was planted in us. What weeds can choke that Word and keep it from growing (v. 21)? Explain.

---

6. In your own words explain how the person who merely listens is different from the one who puts God's Word into practice (vv. 22-25).

7. Why is there a tendency for Christians to listen to and yet not to follow God's Word?

How can you avoid this tendency?

———————————————————————

8. According to verses 26 and 27, how do people who think they are religious differ from those who are truly religious?

———————————————————————

9. Based on what you've read in this chapter, do you think James would be satisfied with good works apart from our listening to and receiving God's Word? Explain.

———————————————————————

10. Give some specific examples of how your religion could become more "pure and faultless" in the sense James has in mind in verse 27.

Ask God to help you become a better listener and doer of his Word.

Now or Later

There is so much to listen to all around us. Take blocks of time over the next few days or weeks to discover what voices and messages are on your mind. Jot them down. Ask God to help you deal with those that distract you from him. Ask him to help you clear your mind and to focus on his Word.

3

Who's the Judge?

James 2:1-13

Labels are found in more places than on soup cans. We put them on people all the time. Funny or dull. Smart or thickheaded. Friendly or cold. There are all kinds of ways we can categorize people. And our categories can have a profound influence on the way we treat people.

GROUP DISCUSSION. What kinds of things make you favor one person more than another?

PERSONAL REFLECTION. Take time to think about the judgmental thoughts and words you have had this week. Confess them to God. Allow yourself to experience his mercy.

As you might suspect, James has a few words to say about favoritism. *Read James 2:1-13.*

---

1. What are some results of showing favoritism (vv. 4, 6, 9, 13)?

---

2. Why should believing in "our glorious Lord Jesus Christ" (v. 1) keep us from showing favoritism?

3. How would you react if someone came into your church who wore sloppy clothes, was dirty or had body odor (vv. 2-4)?

---

4. Why do many people give preferential treatment to those who have money?

---

5. Verse 5 says God has chosen the poor to be rich in faith. Is God guilty of showing favoritism in this way? Explain.

---

6. Is it easier to have faith when you are poor than when you are rich? Explain.

---

7. From a practical standpoint, why was it foolish for early Christians to favor the rich over the poor (vv. 6-7)?

To what extent is James's description of the rich valid today?

8. How can "the royal law" (v. 8) guide our treatment of both poor and rich?

_____

9. How do verses 9-11 emphasize the seriousness of treating people unequally?

_____

10. In what sense is violating one law as serious as breaking every law?

_____

11. What happens to those who show mercy and those who do not (vv. 12-13)?

_____

12. The cross is the ultimate example of mercy triumphing over judgment. How has the mercy you have received there affected the way you interact with others?

Think of ways in which you show favoritism. Ask God to help you change your attitudes and actions.

Now or Later

Who are some people who you avoid or look down on? In what specific ways could you reach out to one such person, do a favor for him or her, or who some others kindness? Bring these ideas to God and make a commitment about which one you will follow up on.

4

Just Works

"It is easier said than done" is a cliché that certainly applies to Christian life. It is much easier to talk about God than to obey him. James said, "Even the demons believe there is one God." But that certainly does not make them Christians! That's why people can have all their doctrine perfectly straight and still miss out on God's will. James helps us stay on target.

GROUP DISCUSSION. What are some ways that we as Christians don't put actions behind our words?

PERSONAL REFLECTION. What has God been asking you to do that you have been trying to ignore?

be a light to Vicky (& other neighbours)

James helps us to see how what we believe needs to be matched by the way we live. *Read James 2:14-26.*

---

1. Retell in your own words the three stories in this passage which illustrate the interaction between faith and works (vv. 15-17, 21-22, 25). Add important details that you remember from the two Old Testament

1. Abraham sacrificing Isaac at the alter
2. telling a poor person to "go in peace, be well" w/o helping them physically
3. Rahab getting messengers out a safe way

stories. (See Genesis 22 and Joshua 2 and 6 to refresh your memory.)

2. In the first story James states clearly that faith without works is dead. What opportunity do you have to show your faith by caring for the poor?

donating to charity shop/food bank homeless shelters

3. Why is mere intellectual agreement to truth not enough (v. 19)?

4. How was Abraham's faith made complete by what he did (vv. 21-24)?

he trusted God enough to sacrifice his son, not merely saying that he trusted Him

5. Describe a time in your life when obedience to God was or could have been at great personal cost to you.

6. How did Rahab's belief affect her (v. 25)?

7. How do your actions demonstrate the reality of your faith?

8. How does James's closing analogy (v. 26) summarize his teaching on faith and actions?

body w/o faith is dead

↓

no use having one w/o the other, meaningless

9. James never says that works without faith can save. What does this imply about faith?

↳ *it's empty, no use w/o putting it into action*

10. How do you respond when the beliefs and actions of others are far apart?

11. In what ways do you need to bring your actions more in line with your beliefs?

Ask God to help you follow through with the works that will reveal your true faith.

Now or Later

Reflect on your life in the past 7-10 days. Write down situations in which what you did or said or thought did not match up with what you believe. Ask God to forgive you, change you and make you more like him. Then write down situations in which you clearly lived out what you believe. Thank God for his faithful work in your life.

5

On Preventing Forest Fires

James 3:1-12

One of the most distressing crises is a fire out of control. The pain of seeing the resulting destruction can be devastating. Personal belongings going up in smoke. The beauty of nature marred. Even the loss of life itself. Hurtful words can have much the same impact.

GROUP DISCUSSION. How have you seen destructive words damage others?

PERSONAL REFLECTION. How have you been hurt by destructive words? Give the pain to God. Let him comfort you.

In this passage James teaches us how our words can bring healing rather than harm. *Read James 3:1-12.*

---

1. List the analogies and comparisons that James uses in these verses to describe the tongue.

2. The author suggests that not many people should become teachers (v. 1). What examples come to your mind of religious leaders or teachers whose lives people judged more strictly than others?

Why were they judged in this way?

_____

3. Why do you think the tongue has such control over our lives as to be compared to a bit and a rudder (vv. 3-4)?

_____

4. What is the point of comparing the tongue to a fire and to a world of evil (vv. 5-6)?

_____

5. Why is it so difficult to control the tongue (vv. 7-8)?

_____

6. In what ways can the tongue poison people and relationships?

7. How do the analogies from nature (springs, trees, vines) highlight the inconsistencies of the tongue?

8. What inconsistencies do you see in the way you talk to others?

9. James has focused primarily on the destructive power of the tongue. In what ways can the tongue also bring refreshment and healing?

10. What in this text gives you added strength and motivation to be more careful with your words?

11. What can you do to give God more praise? Be specific.

12. How can you give more affirmation to those you come in contact with each day?

Ask God to make your tongue a source of life rather than a source of destruction.

Now or Later

James 3:10 says, "Out of the same mouth come praise and cursing. My brothers this should not be." Consider how your words can bring blessing to others. Cultivate a pattern of praise by taking time now to write a letter to someone who needs encouragement and affirmation. Be specific about the good qualities you see in that person and the good things he or she has accomplished.

6

Makers & Breakers of Peace

James 3:13—4:10

Why do the people who love each other the most often fight the most too? Husbands and wives, parents and children, brothers and sisters—it's all too common.

GROUP DISCUSSION. Why do you think that fights and arguments erupt in even the best of families?

PERSONAL REFLECTION. How have you gotten caught up in fighting recently? If conflict continues to be a concern to you, talk to God about it. Ask God to clear your mind of anger and distrust so that you can focus on his healing word.

In this study James helps us to understand the sources of quarrels and the sources of peace. *Read James 3:13—4:10.*

1. In 3:13-18 James discusses earthly and heavenly wisdom. What are the characteristics of each?

2. How might earthly wisdom provoke fights and quarrels?

_____

3. When have you seen the kind of wisdom that comes from heaven help resolve conflict?

_____

4. What would you say is the difference between James's description in 3:17 and being a doormat?

_____

5. What does James say is the source of quarrels (4:1-2)?

_____

6. In contrast, James says we should deal with our desires by asking God for what we want (4:2-3). Why do we sometimes resist or hesitate to ask God for what we want?

_____

7. James says we don't receive even when we ask because we ask with wrong motives (4:3). What might be some examples of right and wrong motives in prayer?

8. What does it mean for us to have "friendship with the world" (4:4)?

9. What else does James say is necessary in order to come to God in prayer (4:4-10)?

10. How do each of these contribute to a humble spirit?

11. James sounds harsh here. Do you think he is being extreme or is he on target? Explain.

12. Are there situations where humility could help you become a source of peace this coming week? Explain.

Take a few minutes to quietly humble yourself before God. Ask him to help you become a peacemaker during the next several days.

Now or Later

Consider the relationships in your life where there is regularly tension, quarrels or hostility. What, if any, are the common traits or patterns in them? What have you learned from this passage that will help you to deal with them?

7

Getting Perspective

"I am the master of my fate. I am the captain of my soul." How subtly we convince ourselves that we control our lives. Sometimes only a crisis or even death itself convinces us otherwise. If we are truly wise and humble, we will listen carefully when James says, "You are a mist that appears for a little while and then vanishes."

GROUP DISCUSSION. Finish the sentence: When I think about my future I _____. You might finish this sentence in a funny way, and then do a second round with a more serious answer.

PERSONAL REFLECTION. Write down specific ways that you have been trying to control your life.

In this study James will help us to identify our attitude toward God, others and the future and to learn how to make them what they should be. *Read James 4:11-17.*

1. What reasons does James give for not slandering or speaking against a Christian brother or sister (vv. 11-12)?

2. How do we tend to build ourselves up by criticizing others?

3. If we judge the law, what does this say about our attitude toward the lawgiver?

4. How can a proper attitude toward God (v. 12) enable us to have a proper attitude toward others?

5. How would you describe the two attitudes toward the future found in verses 13-17?

6. James compares life to a mist (v. 14). How does a sudden death, especially that of a famous person, help us to realize this?

7. How do you feel about your life being like a mist?

_____

8. How does knowing that your life is like a mist affect the way that you think about your future?

_____

9. Is James saying it is wrong to plan for the future? Explain.

_____

10. If you knew you were going to die tomorrow, how would your attitude toward life today be different?

_____

11. In verse 17 James says it is a sin not to do good when we know we should. In what areas of your life do you need to turn your plans over to God's will?

_____

12. How can you cultivate humility in your attitude toward others and toward the future?

Ask God to help you love those around you rather than judge them. Humbly commit your future plans to the Lord.

Now or Later

Pull out your calendar and look at what you have scheduled, or make a list of what you have planned in the next few weeks. Take time to pray through each item. Commit it to God. Put each event under his care and ask him to guide you and others as he desires. Ask God if there are items he wants you to add or to take off your schedule.

8

What Awaits
James 5:1-11

You have probably heard of the young man who cried out, "Lord, I want patience and I want it now!"

GROUP DISCUSSION. Describe some of the many ways that our culture encourages impatience.

PERSONAL REFLECTION. How does the culture set your agenda and determine your lifestyle?

James encourages us in this passage to wait for God, to be patient, and warns us against wanting it all now. *Read James 5:1-11.*

1. Into what two sections is this passage divided, and who is addressed in each?

2. James declares that misery awaits rich people. What crimes have they committed (vv. 1-6)?

3. Is James condemning all rich people? Explain.

_____

4. Do you think of yourself as rich? Why or why not?

_____

5. Look at verses 7-11. How is piling up riches the opposite of patience that waits in faith for God to provide?

_____

6. When are you tempted to hoard rather than to give and wait on God?

_____

7. Why do you think James begins the second section in verse 7 with "Be patient"?

_____

8. James goes on to give three examples of patient people: a farmer, the prophets and Job. How is each an example of patience?

9. In what areas of your life are you impatient?

In what ways could you learn patience from the three examples James mentions?

_____

10. The Lord's coming provides a backdrop for James's word to the rich and to those who suffer. What different reactions would you expect each group to have to the prospect of the Lord's return (vv. 7-9)?

_____

11. How can Christ's return affect such practical matters as our use of wealth and emotional matters as our response to suffering?

Thank God for the practical help James gives in becoming more patient. Ask God to help you apply his message to the areas in your life that need patience.

Now or Later

Many Christians find it a helpful spiritual discipline to regularly write out thoughts and ideas in God's presence, to carry out a conversation with him on paper. It can keep our prayers focused. Having a notebook especially for journaling these thoughts can be meaningful.

Think about your life and journal on the following questions. What in life is most important to me? How does the way I live demonstrate that importance? What is most satisfying to me? How much of my time is spent on that which satisfies? What are my greatest fears? How does the way I live life speak to those fears? How does the way I give demonstrate my trust (or lack of trust) of God?

Reflect on your journaling. Ask God to show you how you sin in hoarding possessions. Ask him to help you know and trust him enough to be willing to wait for him and to give freely.

9

Becoming Whole

James 5:12-20

Broken homes, shattered relationships, damaged emotions—we live in a fragmented and hurting society. As we see all the wounded people around us, we long to help, to offer a healing touch. But although we will spend our lives becoming complete, we will have a hard time helping others unless we are also seeking wholeness ourselves.

GROUP DISCUSSION. Do you pray more when you are in trouble or when things are going well? Explain.

PERSONAL REFLECTION. Journal about two or three wounded people in your life who you would like to help.

In this study James gives us very practical suggestions for becoming whole people and helping others to do the same. *Read James 5:12-20.*

1. How do the instructions in verse 12 reinforce the themes of the tongue (3:1-12) and of patience (5:9-11)?

2. What different kinds of prayer are mentioned in this passage?

3. What experiences have you had with these kinds of prayer in your life?

4. What steps could you take to make at least one of these types of prayer more a part of your life?

5. In verses 14-16 James discusses physical and spiritual healing. What are the steps in this process?

6. How is physical healing connected with forgiveness of sins?

7. Would you call elders or other church leaders for anointing, prayer and confession? Why or why not?

8. How can we provide other opportunities for mutual confession and prayer (v. 16)?

9. How does the Old Testament prophet Elijah illustrate the effectiveness of prayer (vv. 17-18)?

10. Elijah was a person just like us. In what ways do you struggle as you attempt to grow in prayer?

11. According to verses 19-20, how, if at all, are we responsible for one another?

12. Summarize what verses 13-20 teach us about how we can help people to become whole physically, emotionally or spiritually.

13. How would you like to be more involved in this kind of ministry?

Ask God for grace as you minister to others.

Now or Later

The following questions will help you to reflect on what you have learned from James.

What changes have you seen in yourself since you began this study of James?

Why is perseverance so important for Christians?

What one area of your life is in most need of endurance and perseverance?

How have you been encouraged by studying the book of James?

Thank God for what you have learned from studying the book of James.

Leader's Notes

MY GRACE IS SUFFICIENT FOR YOU. (2 COR 12:9)

Leading a Bible discussion can be an enjoyable and rewarding experience. But it can also be *scary*—especially if you've never done it before. If this is your feeling, you're in good company. When God asked Moses to lead the Israelites out of Egypt, he replied, "O Lord, please send someone else to do it!" (Ex 4:13). It was the same with Solomon, Jeremiah and Timothy, but God helped these people in spite of their weaknesses, and he will help you as well.

You don't need to be an expert on the Bible or a trained teacher to lead a Bible discussion. The idea behind these inductive studies is that the leader guides group members to discover for themselves what the Bible has to say. This method of learning will allow group members to remember much more of what is said than a lecture would.

These studies are designed to be led easily. As a matter of fact, the flow of questions through the passage from observation to interpretation to application is so natural that you may feel that the studies lead themselves. This study guide is also flexible. You can use it with a variety of groups— student, professional, neighborhood or church groups. Each study takes forty-five to sixty minutes in a group setting.

There are some important facts to know about group dynamics and encouraging discussion. The suggestions listed below should enable you to effectively and enjoyably fulfill your role as leader.

Preparing for the Study

1. Ask God to help you understand and apply the passage in your own life. Unless this happens, you will not be prepared to lead others. Pray too for the various members of the group. Ask God to open your hearts to the message of his Word and motivate you to action.

2. Read the introduction to the entire guide to get an overview of the entire book and the issues which will be explored.

3. As you begin each study, read and reread the assigned Bible passage to familiarize yourself with it.

4. This study guide is based on the New International Version of the Bible. It will help you and the group if you use this translation as the basis for your study and discussion.

5. Carefully work through each question in the study. Spend time in meditation and reflection as you consider how to respond.

6. Write your thoughts and responses in the space provided in the study guide. This will help you to express your understanding of the passage clearly.

7. It might help to have a Bible dictionary handy. Use it to look up any unfamiliar words, names or places. (For additional help on how to study a passage, see chapter five of *How to Lead a LifeBuilder Study*, IVP, 2018.)

8. Consider how you can apply the Scripture to your life. Remember that the group will follow your lead in responding to the studies. They will not go any deeper than you do.

9. Once you have finished your own study of the passage, familiarize yourself with the leader's notes for the study you are leading. These are designed to help you in several ways. First, they tell you the purpose the study guide author had in mind when writing the study. Take time to think through how the study questions work together to accomplish that purpose. Second, the notes provide you with additional background information or suggestions on group dynamics for various questions. This information can be useful when people have difficulty understanding or answering a question. Third, the leader's notes can alert you to potential problems you may encounter during the study.

10. If you wish to remind yourself of anything mentioned in the leader's notes, make a note to yourself below that question in the study.

Leading the Study

1. Begin the study on time. Open with prayer, asking God to help the group to understand and apply the passage.

2. Be sure that everyone in your group has a study guide. Encourage the group to prepare beforehand for each discussion by reading the introduction to the guide and by working through the questions in the study.

3. At the beginning of your first time together, explain that these studies are meant to be discussions, not lectures. Encourage the members of the group to participate. However, do not put pressure on those who may be hesitant to speak during the first few sessions. You may want to suggest the following guidelines to your group.

☐ Stick to the topic being discussed.

☐ Your responses should be based on the verses which are the focus of the discussion and not on outside authorities such as commentaries or speakers.

☐ These studies focus on a particular passage of Scripture. Only rarely should you refer to other portions of the Bible. This allows for everyone to participate in in-depth study on equal ground.

☐ Anything said in the group is considered confidential and will not be discussed outside the group unless specific permission is given to do so.

☐ We will listen attentively to each other and provide time for each person present to talk.

☐ We will pray for each other.

4. Have a group member read the introduction at the beginning of the discussion.

5. Every session begins with a group discussion question. The question or activity is meant to be used before the passage is read. The question introduces the theme of the study and encourages group members to begin to open up. Encourage as many members as possible to participate and be ready to get the discussion going with your own response.

This section is designed to reveal where our thoughts or feelings need to be transformed by Scripture. That is why it is especially important not to read the passage before the discussion question is asked. The passage will tend to color the honest reactions people would otherwise give because they are, of course, supposed to think the way the Bible does.

You may want to supplement the group discussion question with an icebreaker to help people to get comfortable. See the community section of the *Small Group Starter Kit* (IVP, 1995) for more ideas.

You also might want to use the personal reflection question with your group. Either allow a time of silence for people to respond individually or discuss it together.

6. Have a group member (or members if the passage is long) read aloud the passage to be studied. Then give people several minutes to read the passage again silently so that they can take it all in.

7. Question 1 will generally be an overview question designed to briefly survey the passage. Encourage the group to briefly survey the passage, but try to avoid getting sidetracked by questions or issues that will be addressed later in the study.

8. As you ask the questions, keep in mind that they are designed to be used just as they are written. You may simply read them aloud. Or you may prefer to express them in your own words.

There may be times when it is appropriate to deviate from the study guide. For example, a question may have already been answered. If so, move on to the next question. Or someone may raise an important question not covered in the guide. Take time to discuss it, but try to keep the group from going off on tangents.

9. Avoid answering your own questions. If necessary, repeat or rephrase them until they are clearly understood. Or point out something you read in the leader's notes to clarify the context or meaning. An eager group quickly becomes passive and silent if they think the leader will do most of the talking.

10. Don't be afraid of silence. People may need time to think about the question before formulating their answers.

11. Don't be content with just one answer. Ask, "What do the rest of you think?" or "Anything else?" until several people have given answers to the question.

12. Acknowledge all contributions. Try to be affirming whenever possible. Never reject an answer. If it is clearly off-base, ask, "Which verse led you to that conclusion?" or again, "What do the rest of you think?"

13. Don't expect every answer to be addressed to you, even though this will probably happen at first. As group members become more at ease, they will begin to truly interact with each other. This is one sign of healthy discussion.

14. Don't be afraid of controversy. It can be very stimulating. If you don't resolve an issue completely, don't be frustrated. Move on and keep it in mind for later. A subsequent study may solve the problem.

15. Periodically summarize what the group has said about the passage. This helps to draw together the various ideas mentioned and gives continuity to the study. But don't preach.

16. At the end of the Bible discussion you may want to allow group members a time of quiet to work on an idea under "Now or Later." Then discuss what you experienced. Or you may want to encourage group members to work on these ideas between meetings. Give an opportunity during the session to allow people to talk about what they are learning.

17. Conclude your time together with conversational prayer, adapting the prayer suggestion at the end of the study to your group. Ask for God's help in following through on the commitments you've made.

18. End on time.

Many more suggestions and helps are found in *How to Lead a LifeBuilder Study*.

Components of Small Groups

A healthy small group should do more than study the Bible. There are four components to consider as you structure your time together.

Nurture. Small groups help us to grow in our knowledge and love of God. Bible study is the key to making this happen and is the foundation of your small group.

Community. Small groups are a great place to develop deep friendships with other Christians. Allow time for informal interaction before and after each study. Plan activities and games that will help you to get to know each other. Spend time having fun together—going on a picnic or cooking dinner together.

Worship and prayer. Your study will be enhanced by spending time praising God together in prayer or song. Pray for each other's needs— and keep track of how God is answering prayer in your group. Ask God to help you to apply what you are learning in your study.

Outreach. Reaching out to others can be a practical way of applying what you are learning, and it will keep your group from becoming self-focused. Host a series of evangelistic discussions for your friends or neighbors. Clean up the yard of an elderly friend. Serve at a soup kitchen together, or spend a day working in the community.

Many more suggestions and helps in each of these areas are found in the *Small Group Starter Kit*. You will also find information on building a small group. Reading through the starter kit will be worth your time.

Optional Overview Study

Before the first session you may want to spend a meeting doing an overview of the book of James. Read through the entire book of James (which can be read aloud in about fifteen minutes or silently in five to ten minutes) and then answer the following questions to help give you an overview of the passage.

1. What kind of person do you find James to be?

2. Generally, what is the tone or atmosphere of the letter? (Harsh, kind, easygoing, loving, businesslike, direct, other?) Explain your answer.

3. How do you respond to his tone? Do you like it or not? Why?

4. What main topics are discussed in the letter?

5. What images and examples does James use?

6. What unifying theme, if any, do you see in the letter?

7. How is 1:26-27 expanded on in the rest of the letter?

8. What statements in the letter do you have the most difficulty with, and why?

9. What statements in the letter do you find most exciting and encouraging, and why?

Study 1. James 1:1-18. Dependable or Double-minded.

Purpose: To understand the importance of perseverance when we face trials and temptations.

General note. As the leader you need to work through the study before consulting the leader's notes. You have to deal with the passage personally to lead the group as effectively as possible. So if you have not yet done study 1, do so now. Then come back here.

Finished? Great. Let's hit some practical matters first. Begin the study by taking five minutes to explain that the group will be learning by discussion, by each person's contribution which will be stimulated by a few thought-provoking questions. Review the "Suggestions for Members of a Group Study" (p. 8).

Summarize the key points from the introduction about the person James and the people to whom he wrote his letter. Be sure to mention that he did not follow Jesus until after the resurrection, that he became the head of the early church in Jerusalem, that he was very aware of the potential for conflicts between Jewish-Christians and Gentile-Christians, and that he died a martyr's death.

As James was the head of the church in Jerusalem, he had reason to be authoritative. He didn't live in a hole, however. He was quite aware of human nature and had often dealt with people's problems. Be sure to note how he describes himself in 1:1. What does this say about James? Regarding the recipients of the letter, note that it is not certain if James was writing exclusively to Jewish-Christians or to all Christians outside Palestine. In any case, the letter was not addressed to a specific congregation (as most of Paul's letters were).

Even if each member has a copy of this guide and has read the introduction, you should talk briefly about James and his audience.

This is a key study in this series. Perseverance is a theme which permeates the entire book, though not always explicitly. As James goes on to deal with judging others, the tongue, possessions and other topics, the theme of perseverance is not far in the background.

Question 3. Confusion could arise regarding what perseverance is all about. You may want to make sure your group's understanding of perseverance is adequate. James is not talking about stubbornness or grinning and bearing it.

Question 6. This may elicit questions about the place of doubt in the Christian life. While periods of questioning can be healthy and allow for growth, a life characterized by spiritual indecisiveness is worthless in God's sight. James draws two extremes to make his point.

Question 7. James's second contrast (vv. 9-11) also shows the value of perseverance. When the rich hit a crisis, they turn to God, and this is good. When the poor have something good happen, they seldom give themselves the credit (as the rich might be inclined to do). The poor know it had to come from God, and so they turn to him in thanks. Each situation increases reliance on God.

Thus depending on the makeup of your group, you may want to change question 7 to, "How has good fortune turned you toward God?"

The message here seems to be that the Christian's status in Christ is unaffected by poverty or wealth. Rich Christians are encouraged to find joy not in earthly possessions but in their relationship with Christ. Poor Christians are encouraged to find joy in the fact that in Christ they are exalted. Both are called on to persevere in looking at their situation from God's perspective.

Question 8. People in your group could be at different places in their willingness to discuss how they are affected by their possessions. This question could bring a quick and thoughtful response, a thoughtless response or a reluctance to talk. Be ready to give examples of ways you are dependent and ways that you have been freed from dependence on your possessions.

Question 9. Help the group to look through the passage carefully to see the difference between trials and temptations. The following additional questions could help: What are the results of each (vv. 3-4, 12, 15)? What should the Christian's response be to each (vv. 2, 5-6, 12, 13, 16)? Not all temptations come from trial, but what might turn a trial of verse 12 into a temptation of verse 13?

Question 10. Part of the difference between trials and temptations is the role that God plays in each. In trials we see that while he may not plan them, he does allow them. The reason he allows them is the good that they can produce in the life of Christians if they persevere through the trials. God promises to give wisdom in the midst of the trial to all who ask and believe him when they ask. And finally God promises a crown of life to those who have stood the trial and love him.

On the other hand, God has nothing to do with temptations. God cannot be tempted by evil—it is opposite of his holy nature.

Question 11. The first fruits of the harvest were specifically committed to God as part of the regular thanksgiving of each Israelite (see Lev 23:9-11). The term is often used as a metaphor to signify priority of position and importance in God's sight (for example, Jer 2:3 RSV).

Study 2. Words, Words, Words. James 1:19-27.

Purpose: To learn to listen to others and to the Word, and to put the Word into practice.

Group discussion. Have pencils and pieces of paper ready for everyone. For each round, everyone makes up and writes down a definition of the same word. The leader writes down the real definition. *Oviparous*—producing eggs which hatch after leaving the body of the female. *Foraminifer*—a small one-celled sea animal with a hard shell. *Isochroous*—having the same color in every part. *Bersagliere*—a rifleman.

Question 1. James begins his elaboration of the theme of leading a consistent Christian life by focusing on the place of words in our lives. Your goal as leader is to bring out how we should handle words as Christians and how we should go beyond words to actions.

Question 2. Is anger always a sin? Doesn't Paul say, "Be angry but do not sin" (Eph 4:26 RSV)? Isn't there an appropriate time for anger? When we hear about child abuse, isn't anger justified? These are some questions you could hear from the group members in response to verses 19-20. We are not justified in becoming angry in defense of ourselves. We may, however, find ourselves within the bounds of God's righteous anger when genuine injustice is involved. Even so, God is "compassionate and gracious, slow to anger, abounding in love" (Ps 103:8). We ought to be as well.

Question 3. This question can offer an opportunity for reflection on how people are interacting in the Bible study itself. Are they acting Christianly among themselves? Do some dominate discussion? Do others constantly change the subject or take the group to other parts of Scripture? Does anyone follow up with questions when someone begins to open up with problems or deep concerns? If not, how can the group grow in these areas?

Question 4. "There would seem to be two thoughts underlying what is said in this verse about people's anger. First, people who are full of anger do not practice that kind of conduct which alone is right in God's sight. On the contrary, by allowing free play to passion they render dispassionate, and therefore just, decisions in human affairs impossible. What God requires is that people should 'do justly' (Micah 6:8); and people's anger, fitful and wayward as it is, prevents the fulfillment of this requirement. Secondly, the anger of people prevents God's righteous actions from being vindicated by the Christian; for it becomes more difficult for others to lay hold of the truth that the Judge of all the earth is essentially moral and Himself does what is right, if His servants fail to show righteousness in their conduct" (R.V.G. Tasker, *The General Epistle of James,* Tyndale New Testament Commentary [Grand Rapids, Mich.: Eerdmans, n.d.], p. 50.).

"Therefore, the wise person will be slow to open his or her mouth and even slower to express anger. Indeed James argues, a humble acceptance of the gospel (*the word planted in you*) will mean that one will get rid of all angry expression and all other types of evil even if they are accepted by the world" (G. J. Wenham et al, eds., *New Bible Commentary* [Downers Grove, Ill.: InterVarsity Press, 1994], p. 1359.).

One should not have to look far to find in one's own life an example of anger that does not result in the righteous life which God desires. It is difficult to give concrete examples from our own lives of sin and failure. And some in your group may be victims of anger. Try to create an environment of safety, free of judgment in order for the topic of anger and the damage done by it to be discussed, while keeping in mind of hope and forgiveness that is an integral part of the gospel message and that word planted in us.

Question 5. Throughout this passage, we read about weeds—such as anger, not listening to God's Word and to each other, moral filth, evil and not obeying God's Word—that choke God's Word and keep it from growing within us. Help the group to identify these first and then to continue to discuss weeds from their own experience that may not be explicitly mentioned here.

Question 6. "The perfect law" mentioned in James 1:25 is the new covenant. Christ completed the old covenant, setting us free to be in harmony with God and with ourselves (see Jer 31:31-34 and Mt 5:17).

Question 8. Some are likely to object to James's description of pure and genuine religion in verse 27. Note however that he does not say this is all that true religion is. Nevertheless, it does cover things pretty well. The phrase *orphans and widows* is a general reference to all in need of help, while to keep oneself from being polluted by the world encourages us to adopt godly values, attitudes and virtues.

Question 10. Help the group think of specific people in their lives that need their care. What are the different ways people can be in distress like an orphan or a widow? Be prepared to share ways you need to grow in not being polluted by the world.

Study 3. Who's the Judge? James 2:1-13.

Purpose: To learn to treat others as God treats us.

Group discussion: Some possible answers (if people are honest) might include: "If they have personalities I can get along with." "How much they accept me." "What they have accomplished in life." "How they look." As with all opening questions, accept all answers without comment—except to help people clarify or expand on their answers. Wait till later in the study to apply James's teaching to these initial responses.

Question 3. Even if your church or fellowship group has a large number of poor folk in it, some people have very strong ideas about what is appropriate Sunday attire. Otherwise you may want to skip this question.

Question 5. Is God guilty of favoritism? Perhaps he is just trying to even the odds, so to speak, compensating the poor spiritually for what they might lack materially.

If God has chosen the poor (see Ps 140:12; Prov 19:17; Lk 1:52-53; 6:20-25), does this mean the rich (and most people ,in industrialized countries are rich compared to the rest of the world) are automatically rejected by God? If such a question is raised, direct the group back to James for the answer. You might also direct them to 1:9-11 where James points out how God helps both poor and rich to trust in him.

Some might also suggest that James is speaking of the poor in spirit in verse 5. Yet the context of 2:1-4 and the way the poor are dishonored as described in 2:6-7 indicate he means the materially poor.

Question 6. It is easy to depend on our wealth—rather than God—to take care of us (when we have it). Christians who are poor materially have nothing else to depend on—so believing in God might come more easily.

Question 9. Verses 10-11 might also raise some objections. Try not to get sidetracked on whether stealing a pencil is as bad as murder. Others might also say, "Well, if I'm condemned for a lie, I might as well commit adultery." James's point is that in the eyes of the law, a transgression is a transgression. This emphasizes the seriousness of acting in a prejudiced manner.

Question 10. This question gets to the heart of the issue raised in the first question. Even a "minor" sin is serious, not just because a rule is violated but because the special relationship God intends to have with human beings is broken.

Questions 11-12. While James says very little directly about Christ in his letter, it is shot through with Christ's teaching and with a theology that is rooted in the center of the Christian faith. In this case, mercy triumphs over judgment for each sinner who, condemned to eternal punishment (judgment), is granted forgiveness (mercy) by accepting the substitution of Christ's death for his own. Thus we should act as those who have been set free and not hold tightly to our judgment of (unwillingness to forgive) others. This, of course, is the very teaching we find in the Lord's Prayer (forgive as we forgive others—Mt 6:12) and in Christ's parable of the unmerciful steward (Mt 18:21-35).

Study 4. Just Works. James 2:14-26.

Purpose: To see how what we believe needs to be matched by the way we live.

Group discussion. If you have people in your group who aren't Christians, you could simply ask, What are some ways that we don't put actions behind our words?

General note. This could well be your most controversial discussion in James. This passage has certainly raised more questions about the book of James than anything else. It was primarily because of the seeming emphasis on salvation by works that Martin Luther virtually booted this epistle out of his Bible. Many people mistakenly assume that James is in a direct debate with Paul and that the two are taking opposing positions. Yet such is not the case. James's emphasis is that true faith is evidenced by works, not that works alone is sufficient or that works and faith in combination save. Verses 18 and 22 make this point as well. When in verse 24 James says, "not by faith alone," he is speaking of the kind of faith the demons possess—mere intellectual assent, which cannot save. Such a position does not contradict Paul at all, who made a similar point. Compare James 2:14 with Titus 1:16 and Ephesians 2:8-10.

Many Christians are doctrinally orthodox but fail to be orthodox in the outworking of their faith. Their faith is all in their head and not in their actions. This is the sort of person James seeks to touch. And this should be the emphasis you give to the study as well. While the whole book helps us put our faith into practice, this passage specifically aims to controvert the fallacy that right doctrine and "nice" words are sufficient. Real faith is always indicated by works. If there are no works, the faith is not real. It cannot save. Rather, the kind of faith that can and does save always results in Christian action. This was the case with Abraham as well as with Rahab.

Question 3. Many people know the doctrines of Christianity and may even believe them to be true. But they may have never made a commitment to Jesus Christ, placing their trust in him as their Savior and Lord.

Question 4. According to the *New Bible Commentary*:

> James now offers to give scriptural proof of what he has been arguing. Abraham was considered righteous or 'declared to be righteous' in Gn. 22:12, when God says, 'Now I know that you fear God'. This was on account of his deed in preparing to offer Isaac. In other words, Abraham's decision to follow God and put his trust in him was so firm that when faced with the greatest of tests he followed through and resolutely obeyed, whatever the cost.
>
> There is, however, more than this in the text. The phrase *what he did* in the NIV should be 'from his works [or deeds].' Notice that it is 'works' plural not 'work'. James is not thinking of the one deed of Abraham. In Jewish eyes the offering of Isaac was the end of a long string of obedience beginning in Genesis 12:1. Their question was, Why did God command the answer offering of Isaac and then not make Abraham not actually do it? Their was that since Abraham had been obedient so many times before, including, according to their stories, being great in care for the poor, God righteously rewarded his works in Gn. 22 by sparing Isaac. The release of Isaac comes, not after a single deed, but after a lifetime of obedience.
>
> James now observes that faith and actions (or deeds or works) cannot be separated. Faith which is only in the mind is not yet complete. It becomes complete when it results in a decision of the will and is carried out in action. (p. 1361)

Question 7. Many groups will be concerned about whether or not James contradicts Paul on the issue of faith and works. If you anticipate that your group will want to discuss this, you may want to add the following question between questions 7 and 8: James says, "A person is justified by what he does and not by faith alone" (v. 24). How can this be reconciled with Paul's teaching that we are justified by faith and not by works (Rom 4:4-5; Eph 2:8-9)? Note that, in addition to the different way Paul and James may be using the word *faith,* they may also be using the word *justification* in different ways. For Paul it means to be declared righteous. For James it may mean to prove the validity of faith.

Question 9. This question can be crucial if some in the group believe James is advocating salvation by works alone. Don't miss it.

Question 11. Give people time to reflect and to share if they desire. If those present have a hard time thinking of any discrepancies between their beliefs and their actions, maybe the group should discuss how each can observe his or her own actions more critically.

Study 5. On Preventing Forest Fires. James 3:1-12.

Purpose: To learn how our words can bring healing rather than harm.

Question 1. Please just have the group list the analogies and comparisons to the tongue right now with no further discussion. They will be covered more thoroughly throughout the study.

James has structured this passage to explain the substantial responsibilities and risks taken by teachers. James does this through a series of analogies which explain the power of the tongue (vv. 3-4), the difficulty in controlling the tongue (vv. 5-8) and the gross inconsistencies possible with the tongue (vv. 9-12). The questions themselves are thus structured around these explanations. Obviously James's words apply far beyond teachers. We can all find ourselves in this passage. Your task is to help the group members do just this.

Question 2. Not only do teachers have responsibilities to teach what is right and true and what is not, they also will be judged by the standards they themselves tell others to live up to. That is why it is so scandalous when we hear of religious leaders who have fallen victim to greed or lust or lying. We expect more from them (as does the world) because they are the ones who are upholding God's high standards of truth and love. Politicians or entertainers who engage in the same sinful conduct are not generally judged nearly so harshly by the public.

At the same time, James makes the point throughout this passage that the tongue is a powerful instrument, immensely difficult to control, though very potent when it is controlled (like a rudder on a ship or a bit in a horse's mouth). Since words are the chief tool of teachers, they are more responsible than most to use words correctly and helpfully.

Question 6. You may be able to skip this question if the topic of destructive criticism has been adequately covered in previous questions.

Question 7. According to the *New Bible Commentary:*

The insulting of a person, made in God's image, is like insulting God Himself. This . . . is a type of hypocrisy.

James gives two examples to drive this point home. The first is . . . a stream flowing down the valley wall. One journeys to it hoping for water. Sometimes the water is fresh and good. Sometimes it is full of minerals (salt) and is undrinkable. But one thing is sure, the two types of water will not flow out of the same spring. Likewise one does not get a different type of fruit from a tree or vine than that which grows according to its nature. The implication of the is argument is that if we are speaking insults, or curses, that is our nature. Our praises of God are a cover-up, a type of hypocrisy. (p. 1363)

Question 9. This is an important question. Proper use of the tongue is not just controlling the negative but funneling the positive to positive use—just as a tamed horse can be put to constructive purposes.

Questions 11-12. Look up *praise* in a Bible dictionary if you can't define it adequately yourself. Most people would be hard pressed to praise God in prayer for five minutes. Why? Most people would be hard pressed to praise even a close friend for five minutes. Why? How can this be overcome? You can only help your group grapple honestly with these issues through follow-up questions if you have dealt with them in your own life. Go back and see if you are satisfied with your own answers.

Study 6. Makers & Breakers of Peace. James 3:13—4:10.

Purpose: To understand the sources of quarrels and the sources of peace.

General note. Everyone gets into arguments, some more frequently than others. James is seeking to identify the sources of quarrels and how they can be avoided. The sources are envy and self-ambition. The solution is humility before God and others. Keep these two things in mind as you lead.

Studies 6 and 7 could quite easily be entitled "Humility 1" and "Humility 2." The passage is split simply because it would be too long to discuss adequately in one hour. Study 6 approaches humility from the perspective of making and breaking peace. To be a peacemaker you need humility. Study 7 approaches humility more directly. How do you view yourself in relation to God, others and the future? Do you put others down to build yourself up? Do you feel competent to do good on your own?

You might think of this study as being in two halves—3:13-18 and 4:1-10. Humility is the implied solution to quarrels in the first half (accepting God's wisdom rather than your own). It is made explicit, however, in the second half.

Question 2. Help the group to look at what provokes fights and quarrels. Envy and selfish ambition are ever present and often at the core of them. Envy and ambition, that wisdom which "does not come down from heaven," do the opposite to making peace—they cause disorder and every evil practice.

Question 3. When answering this question help the group to look at each characteristic of wisdom (pure, peace-loving, considerate, submissive, full of mercy and so on) and talk about how each would contribute to resolving conflict.

Question 7. The overall wrong motive in prayer is seeking our own will rather then God's will or his wisdom. Our own desires or pleasure is what we seek. God's goal is not to give us what we demand or to meet our every impulse. His will is that we learn to love what he loves. It is not that God does not want people to have pleasure but he wants us to take pleasure in what he knows is good.

Question 9. The difficulty in translating verse 5 is evidenced by the fact that the NIV offers three possibilities, none of which makes very much sense. Likely the verse means either that God's indwelling Spirit and sinful envy are not compatible in God's people (a thought very similar to that of verse 4) or that God is a jealous husband (Ex 20:5; 34:14; Deut 4:24) who will not tolerate divided loyalty by his bride.

Question 10. You might choose to lead the group through each but time will probably be short so you can pick out those that you think are most important—or ask the group to do so. For instance, why might choosing to be a friend of God rather than a friend of the world, contribute to a humble spirit? For one thing, it probably will involve giving up what the world has to offer or thinks is important.

Question 11. Don't feel as though you need to defend James for being harsh. Be willing to be open to a variety of opinions. Some may think he is offering a measured response. Others may think he is being harsh—and appropriately so. Still others may feel he has gone over the top. But to try to get the group to focus on what they think James is ultimately trying to achieve and what they believe his basic points to be.

Question 12. Please make sure there is time for this final application question.

Study 7. Getting Perspective. James 4:11-17.

Purpose: To identify our attitudes toward God, others and the future and to learn how to make them what they should be.

Question 1. If there is some question about how we judge the law (v. 11), you could ask, "In what sense are we judging the law when we speak against others?"

To criticize another person is to break the command to love one's neighbor, or to say in effect, "I have decided (judged) that the law really isn't a good one and doesn't apply in this case. For, you see, I am above the law (being the judge of when it applies and when it doesn't) and am free to break it by being critical of another person."

Questions 6-7. The point of the mist analogy is not that life is insignificant but that it is temporary. Note that it is set in contrast to verse 13, which expresses the attitude that life will go on indefinitely and that I am in control.

Some group members may have never considered that their life is temporary. In fact, they may even refuse to accept this during the study itself: "Oh, I never think about that. You can't live like there's no tomorrow." Be ready to bring the discussion back to what James says, asking the group to look to the passage for answers if no conclusions develop.

Questions 8-9. In the IVP New Testament Commentary *James*, George Stulac writes:

> It would be a deformed spirituality to apply this by refusing to do any planning; 4:15 affirms the validity of planning to do this or that. Motyer writes, "James is not trying to banish planning from our lives, but only that sort of self-sufficient, self important planning that keeps God for Sunday but looks on Monday to Saturday as mine". The spirituality James wants for us is a humble reliance on God which flows from knowing that one is in reality dependent on God for every moment. It is yet another example of how James would envision the grace-reliance in our lives. ([Downers Grove, Ill: InterVarsity Press, 1993]), pp. 160.)

Question 11. Stulac continues:

> Suddenly James shifts his emphasis from whether we *know* God's will
> to whether we *do* God's will. Verse 17 seems at first not to fit the
> thrust of the paragraph. . . . He may have made a jump in his line of
> thought without articulating the intervening steps, but it is entirely
> consistent with the rest of the letter for James to tell his readers to
> carry out their inward attitude with outward actions. In fact, James
> capsulizes in this one verse much of what he has already taught in
> the letter. His double use of the verb *poieo* (to do and doesn't do)
> reminds his readers succinctly of his earlier emphasis on doing the
> work of God (1:22-25). The picture of one *who knows the good he*
> *ought to do and doesn't do it* recalls the earlier picture of one who finds
> the brother or sister in need but does not do the good that ought to
> be done. (p. 161)

Study 8. What Awaits. James 5:1-11.

Purpose: To see the importance of patience in our lives, especially as it
relates to hoarding.

Question 1. This passage discusses two seemingly disconnected topics—
hoarding (coveting, materialism) and patience. Your concern as group
leader is to highlight the ways these two actually intertwine.

This is a very important observation question. Do not skip it because it
may seem too easy. Make sure the group knows that the second section
begins with verse 7. The first section is addressed to rich people who do
not know God. The fact that they do not know God is obvious by how they
live, what they do with their riches and how they treat people. The second
section is written to those James calls "brothers"—fellow believers. Those
who the author encourages to grow in patience. To grow in what is
important.

Question 3. Being wealthy is not the issue with James—but how the
wealthy act and what they do with their wealth. In this passage James is
talking about the wealthy outside the church. "These people are not only
failing the test of having wealth, but they are also the source of some of the
pressure on the church as they take advantage of poor Christians either
because they are poor or because they are Christians or both" *(New Bible*

Commentary, p. 1365).

Question 4. It is always possible to think of people who are richer than you. That is part of the seductiveness of wealth. You can never have enough to satisfy or be ahead of everyone else. Try to be honest about your wealth in relationship to the world as a whole, to your nation, your city and your neighborhood.

Question 6. This may throw some people. But don't be put off. Persist in seeking a response. Essentially hoarding means you can't wait to have something or that things control you (have priority in your life). You must possess all you can because you are afraid you might never get what you want or that you might lose it later. Patience, by definition, waits. It is an act of faith to believe that God is good, that he will provide. We don't have to anxiously work because we fear he won't come through. We can relax in confidence in him.

Question 7. Here is connection number two between hoarding and patience. Hoarding creates hardships for others. It makes it necessary for them to be patient, to wait for God's justice to prevail.

Question 8. Feel free to take time on this question. Obviously, a farmer can't harvest in the spring. He has to wait until fall. Likewise, if a prophet foretells what will happen in the future, by definition it won't happen now. He has to wait to be proven correct. (Hebrews 11:32-38 could also offer you a quick summary of the patience and triumphs of the prophets.) Job endured great suffering, losing his possessions, his children and his health. He had to wait for God to vindicate him, to show that he was not suffering as punishment for sin.

Question 9. The key to application lies in these questions. For example, it was what Job knew and learned about God that gave him his patience. The same can be true for us. If we know God is completely generous, wise and sovereign, for example, we can trust him to give us all we need at the time best for us. We need not pile up riches impatiently, untrustingly.

Question 10. Many Christians today look forward excitedly to Christ's return, little realizing that the judgments he will deal out may be on them and their nation. Be aware if such misconceptions are common in your group.

Question 11. Not only does God rule time and require us to be good stewards of it, he also rules over wealth and requires our obedience to his will in all use of it. Being reminded of Christ's return should encourage us as Christians that we need not nor should we hold on to our possessions as others do. Life will not always be as it is now. The promise of Christ's return should free us and encourage us toward total obedience in the use of our material possessions. It will not always be as it appears to be now for the rich who ignore God and put their confidence in their possessions. "James wants his readers to understand that suffering enters the believer's life; perseverance is the believer's response; blessing comes from the Lord who is full of compassion and mercy" (George Stulac, *James*, p. 174).

Study 9. Becoming Whole. James 5:12-20.

Purpose: To grow in prayer and in helping others.

General note. Don't be deceived. This is not a short study. Even though it covers only eight verses, you will need to gauge your time carefully. Several potentially controversial topics lurk in this passage—faith healing, and the church's role in it, is most notable among them. The place of prayer in one's life also deserves time so the group members can get the concrete help needed in weak areas. Set a pastoral tone for this section of James dealing with the needs (physical, emotional and spiritual) of those in the body.

Question 1. Verse 12 can be seen as the beginning of a review of themes covered so far in the letter, such as the tongue, faith, sin and the like. For example, James reinforces the theme of patience in that taking the Lord's name in vain is one of the most frequent manifestations of impatience.

James wants our yes to be yes and our no to be no so we do not make impetuous, exaggerated commitments to God either because we want to impress others (not very humble) or because we are trying to impress God and manipulate him into doing what we want (not very patient).

Question 2. This is an overview question of the rest of James 5. Allow time for the group to think through the different kinds of prayer that are spoken of throughout the passage. Let them go as broad as they desire in what they call prayer.

The kinds of prayer mentioned are:

v. 13 **Petition.** When we are in trouble we are urged to call upon God for help. **Praise.** When we are happy it is fun to pray prayers of praise to God. That, however should not be the only time we praise him.

v. 14 **Prayers for healing**

v. 16 **Prayers of confession**

Prayers of supplication. Praying for others as they confess their sins.

v. 16 **Prayers of righteous people**

v. 17 **Earnest prayer**

v. 18 **Prayers for specific acts of nature—to honor and glorify God**

v. 20 **Supplication.** Praying for brothers and sisters who wander from truth.

Question 5. It is important to note that the sick person initiates the healing process for several reasons: (1) psychologically people are most likely to receive help if they see their own need; (2) we should be cautious about forcing help on those who do not want it; (3) James makes it clear that this is one permissible way to deal with illness (there is no must in the sentence). It is hoped that these points will flow from the questions here as the discussion progresses.

Olive oil was used both internally and externally for medicinal purposes. It was also used in religious ceremonies of consecration (Ex 29:2) and purification (Lev 14:10-18). It symbolized gladness, comfort and spiritual nourishment.

Question 6. In *James* George Stulac comments on prayer for healing and sin.

James introduces the mention of sin at the end of 5:15 in the context of praying for the sick person: *If he has sinned, he will be forgiven.* It is a conditional clause and the connection between sin and illness is a possibility, not a necessity in every case. The implication is that the physical illness and the guilt may be interwoven, and the cure promised in 5:16 seems to encompass both physical and spiritual healing. We are to pray as repentant sinners asking for a comprehensive healing of our lives.

This passage helps us to realize what a dramatic transformation of relationships James envisions. He points out the oneness that we have with each other because of our common need for forgiveness. If we consciously stand together before God as sinners needing grace and wanting righteousness, that stance has compelling application to our relationships. Instead of judging each other, we will be driven to confess to each other. (pp. 182-183)

Question 7. Not all churches today have elders but most all of them have spiritual leaders that could be called. This passage is communicating one way for the sick to be prayed for. We believe there are other means for this kind of prayer and confession within the Christian community. Small groups can lay hands on and pray for sick members of their group. Special prayer meetings can be called to pray for the sick.

Question 8. The whole book of James brings us to the point of providing opportunities for mutual confession and prayer. If we follow the instructions that James gives us for relating to each other and prayerfully work at developing the attitudes toward each other that he describes, we should be providing safe environments for mutual confession and prayer.

James is first directing us back to God in faith with a reliance on him in prayer. He tells us not to play favorites, not to attack each other verbally and not to judge each other. He lets us know that we are all sinners and need to come together to God in repentance and prayer. How can we place guilt on someone else when we are sinners? Surely when I know the depths of my sin I can openly receive, love and pray for my brothers and sisters as they confess their sins to me.

Prayer partnerships, small groups, friends who meet to read the Word and pray, are all contexts for mutual prayer and confession.

Question 9. See 1 Kings 17:1; 18:1, 42.

Question 11. In this day of individualism in Western culture the description in verses 19-20 may seem foreign. However, accountability to one another, encouraging one another in the faith and even going after someone who is wandering from the faith is not only encouraged here but has great reward. What is more worthwhile than saving a someone from death and covering a multitude of sin?

> There is no distinction made here between evangelizing a non-Christian and discipling one who believes. In either context, James wants his readers to see the urgency of bringing people to repentance. This is why he has written so severely to people whom he loves so dearly as 'brothers.' . . .
>
> This is what Douglas Webster calls 'the work of spiritual direction.' It is a ministry of cutting through the deceptive complexities of a relativistic culture and setting before others a clear path of obedience. It is a ministry that simplifies and clarifies life by defining godly commitments and directing people toward maturity. It is a ministry

of mutually discipling in the church, and it is based on one of the most crucial principles for effective church discipline: that the whole church is called to exercise discipline, not just pastors or elders. . . .

These are the realities of life with which James concludes his letter: There is truth to be followed. There is death to be avoided. There is ministry to give to each other. James has called us to serve both God and sinners." (George Stulac, *James*, p. 189)

Optional Review Study.
You may want to spend a session reviewing the content of the whole book of James. You can use these questions in conjunction with the questions in the "Now and Later" section of study 9.

1. What unifying theme, if any, did you see in James?

2. Why is perseverance so important for Christians (see especially 1:1-18)?

3. How is James's view of religion (1:26-27) developed in the rest of the letter?

4. Some people think James is an antifaith letter. How would you respond to that claim?

5. What examples does James give of faith and actions working together?

6. How does 5:7-20 act as a summary of the letter?

7. From your study of James, what one area of your Christian life would you say is in most need of endurance and consistency?

8. What steps are you taking or will you take to work on that?

Andrew T. Le Peau was the associate publisher for editorial at InterVarsity Press where he worked from 1975 to 2016. Phyllis J. Le Peau is an area director for InterVarsity Christian Fellowship in metro Chicago. They are also the coauthors of the LifeBuilder Bible Studies Ephesians *and* Grandparenting. *Phyllis is the author of the LifeBuilder* Acts, *as well as over a dozen other Bible study guides.*